My Name is Legion
For We Are Many

Edited & Compiled by S. Connolly

DB Publishing
USA

Published by DB Publishing - 2012

ISBN 1470081725

Editorial Staff: S. Connolly and Tenebrae Accedit

Cover Design: G. Bradshaw

Book Design: S. Connolly

This book is dedicated to the chosen ones who traverse the darker paths and dare to explore the great Abyss, led by the Daemonic Divine.

Editor's Foreword

Thank you for picking up a copy of this book. When I first started this project I knew that there wouldn't be a great deal of investors and I knew we'd have a hard time finding contributors. After all, who really wants to share their story with the world? Especially with a topic so intimate and as a personal as a relationship with the divine that is so taboo, that history has seen countless people shunned and even murdered for it.

But many brave souls did step forward and on the following pages you'll read their stories of self-discovery and personal truth. Stories all of us who take the path less traveled can relate to. Stories those who choose more mainstream paths may not know of. It was my hope, in compiling this book, that we could educate others by showing that we're normal people just like everyone else. We walk among you. There are many of us.

For those who tread this path with us, it is my hope this book will inspire you and let you know that you are among kindred.

What I learned from compiling this book is those who have chosen a darker path are very well educated individuals whose choice was not blind or coerced by any one thing. I realized the first step of any journey always begins with a question and each answer brings a new question. If we follow the questions and their answers and subsequent questions, before we know it we're on a path moving toward the unknown.

The stories on the following pages are true. Tenebrae and I have edited them minimally. We wanted them to retain the true essence of their authors. When we did edit, it was for clarity, some grammar, punctuation, and spelling. Every change was made consciously. Everything we didn't change was done consciously as well. Please keep that in mind when reading.

~S. Connolly

An Introduction

By S. Connolly & Tenebrae Accedit

There are many myths and misconceptions about Satanism, Daemon Worship, and "Dark" Paganisms.

In recent years the *National Child Safety Council* put out a booklet about drug abuse that is often sent home with grade school and middle school children. In this book is a section about Satanism that propagates the most common misconceptions people have about Satanism. Clearly it's all erroneous hold-over information from the Satanic Ritual Abuse (SRA) panic of the 1990's. Refuting these common misconceptions seemed an apt way to start this book, so the gentle reader is at least moderately informed about the vast amount of misinformation out there.

Misconception: All pagans and those who follow darker paths are Satanists.

Truth: This is false. Satanists worship Satan, or venerate Satan in some way. Demonolaters aren't necessarily Satanists. Some can be if they venerate Satan, but not all do. Finally, pagans of a "darker path" are generally not Satanists either. They can be if they venerate Satan, but not always. Now I realize people like to lump us all together, but you can't do that. Just like there are numerous denominations of Christianity, so are their numerous denominations of Satanism, Daemonolatry, and darker pagan paths. By "darker" pagan paths I mean those who might work with or worship darker deities or who are simply traditional witches who see nothing wrong with throwing a curse or ten and who don't ascribe to the Wiccan Rede. We're not all the same.

Misconception: Witches are Satanists.

Truth: While there may be Satanic Witches (I have met a few), most Witches are NOT Satanists. For that matter, not all Witches are Wiccan either. Again, there are many denominations of Witchcraft.

Misconception: "The Baphomet, the Ankh, 666, the Star and Moon, Hexagram, Horned Hand, Swastika and Inverted Cross are all symbols of Satanism."

Truth: Yes, the Baphomet and Inverted Cross imagery do have a place in *some* Satanisms. 666 is often used tongue-in-cheek. The rest of these symbols have nothing to do with Satanism specifically whatsoever. That isn't to say there haven't been fringe groups that combined Satanism with Neo-Nazi beliefs (that has happened). And let's face it, most of us are guilty of giving the horned hand at least once or twice (who hasn't?). My guess is the Ankh, Hexagram, and 666 connection to Satanism all came from Thelema (Aleister Crowley) which the author(s) of this particular Child Safety Council booklet erroneously believed was the same thing as Satanism. Thelema (another minority religion with several denominations) is also not Satanism.

Misconception: "Once a person joins a satanic cult, it is extremely difficult to get out of it."

Truth: Nonsense. With all legitimate groups a person can leave at any time. Not to mention the majority of those who practice Satanism, Daemon Worship, or "Darker" Pagan paths are solitary (i.e. don't belong to a group).

Misconception: "Satanic cults recruit kids."

Truth: Most established covens or groups do not allow initiation of anyone under the age of eighteen.

Misconception: "Satanism lures in unsuspecting teenagers by offering sex, drugs, and power in exchange for silence and loyalty."

Truth: Once again, most of the established covens

and groups do not allow initiation to anyone under eighteen. At most a 16-18 year old may be allowed to participate in study groups or online forums. While some groups may practice sex magick among consenting adults (it's a rarity), most do not. Many groups also actively discourage drug use. Not to mention you're far more likely to meet or live next to a lone Satanist (what we call solitary) than you are groups of them.

Misconception: "Satanists practice sacrifice, rape, torture, and the drinking of urine and blood."

Truth: None of the Satanic groups I know of (and I know of quite a few), and none of the solitary Satanists, Daemonolaters, or dark Pagans I know do any of these things. If there are groups or individuals who practice such things they would be an exception rather than a rule. Now some traditional forms of Daemonolatry do have a blood imbibement rite, but it consists of drops of blood added to the ritual wine. That's not quite the same thing as drinking blood.

Misconception: "Satanism is the opposite of Christian beliefs."

Truth: There are many different types of Satanism, Daemonolatry, and Dark Paganism. The general rule of thumb is if you've seen it in a Hollywood movie, chances are it isn't true or correct.

Misconception: Satanists all listen to heavy metal music, wear black, and look like freaks.

Truth: Some of them may choose to listen to metal or wear black (wearing black and listening to metal no more makes one a Satanist, Daemonolater, or Dark Pagan than owning a liquor store makes one an alcoholic), but many do not. Some of us enjoy all kinds of music. Some may even listen to opera, own their own homes, drive new cars, and you wouldn't be able to pick them out of a lineup of Sunday School teachers. Imagine that.

Misconception: Satanists are out to take over the world and destroy Christianity.

Truth: Most of us who practice minority religions like Satanism, Daemonolatry, or darker pagan paths are just trying to make a life for ourselves and our families. I have yet to meet anyone who aspires (or has the means) to take over the world in the name of Satan (or any other "dark" deity for that matter). Most Satanists, Daemonolaters and "Dark" Pagans are content to be left alone to worship and believe as they wish. I have yet to meet a dark pagan who believes that we should convert others to our respective religions. Such doctrines seem to be the antithesis of most dark pagan, Satanic, and Demonolatry based paths. Many of us contend that we were chosen for our path. You either have a calling to the dark arts and the Daemonic Divine or you do not. You can't force a calling.

Misconception: Satanism is all about Anton LaVey.

Truth: Again, there are many types of Satanism and Satanism was actually around longer than LaVey. He just made his personal version of it popular with the mass distribution of his *Satanic Bible*.

Misconception: The star itself is a pentagram!

Truth: A Pentegram has a circle around it. Without the circle it is a Pentalpha.

Sharon D.

Age 55
Denver, CO
Retired Law Enforcement

My story is not typical. Back in the late eighties I was working as an occult crimes investigator for a tri-state area. This was during the era we called the "Satanic Panic" where there were numerous claims of Satanic Ritual Abuse (SRA). It was my job to go over the entire crime scene, evidence, and pictures, and decipher any symbolism or signs of occult activity for clues as to what occult group was behind it. We never did find any genuine occult or Satanic crimes.

During the course of my work, I realized that the reference materials and training I was given to do my job was all very slanted and incorrect. During my time at this job, I had the opportunity to actually interview and speak with numerous occultists of various paths, and I began collecting my own library of reference material written by the people who were actually practicing these occult religions. I began to learn that what was in the departmental approved research materials and what was in the books written by the occultists themselves didn't match up.

Due to this serious discrepancy, I began researching the authors of the approved "expert" materials, only to discover the foremost authors of these materials were Christians, or at least coming from a Judeo-Christian worldview, and clearly had no understanding of the occult at all. Their understanding was based more on Hollywood fiction than reality. I was intrigued by the material I was reading and before I knew it I had amassed a good sized library. People in my department came to regard me as more of an expert than some of the expert lecturers who toured the country that were educating law enforcement professionals on the "signs" of occult crime and ritual abuse.

It was during one particular investigation, the alleged satanic slaughtering of a black cat (which turned out to be neighborhood kids),that led me to interview people in the neighborhood, and where I also ended up meeting a couple, who, after we'd spoken a few times, revealed to me they were practicing Demonolaters. I was intrigued by the idea of demon worship. They invited me to one of their study groups. So, in my off time, I began attending the study groups, and finally accepted the fact that I wasn't just interested in occult religions, but I'd actually found one that resonated with me enough to make me want to practice it. I was in my early thirties and still had kids at home at the time. I didn't really share with my family what I was doing at first. I started by converting my home office to do dual duty as a private meditation and prayer space by putting up a small altar.

This didn't go unnoticed by my husband and two oldest children, who asked me about it over breakfast one morning. That's when I broke the news and told them that their once non-religious (agnostic perhaps) wife and mother had converted to a religion called Demonolatry.

Because my family wasn't religious to begin with it wasn't a very big deal, and my husband and the kids seemed to take it in stride. Eventually two of my four children decided to share in my beliefs. While I did belong to a group for many years, for me Demonolatry has always been a very personal, solitary practice. Once the local group dissolved I continued on my own and chose not to re-join a group when a new one rose from the ashes of the first, even though I still have friends I keep in contact with within said group.

My relationship with the Daemons is between me and my understanding of the Daemonic, which for me, is another way of discussing the divine intelligence. One of my children has chosen to raise their children within Demonolatry, and I am fine with that. I did eventually add some magickal practices to my personal Demonolatry and I still practice it to this day. I am not completely out of the closet with my extended family or former co-workers, as I am retired from law enforcement now.

The only people who know are immediate family and close friends. I'm comfortable with that.

F.V. Fargas

Age 21
Romania (Bucharest)
http://www.lulu.com/spotlight/FVFargas
http://fvfargas.wordpress.com?

I do not know if Egotrism can be a religious path, but it is certainly a movement of religious essence. As a life guide for myself, it turned out to be more than just an ideology, it became my own religious path. I believe that everyone must be aware of the importance of his religion in his/her life. Religion should not be taken as a group in which you choose to join, in order to find a place in society. From my point of view, religion is the destiny of each man's soul, it is his way of life, and the highway to death. Yes, religion can change your way of life and way of thinking. Unlike atheism, religion offers you something more. It offers you a new theory, a "new" pair of eyes, which will help you see the importance of spirituality in life and of the spiritual evolution.

Of course, every religion is different. Every

religion shows you a different image on life, on the spirit, and on yourself. Christianity is different from Satanism, Judaism is different from Hinduism, and so on. Also, each person is different from another, and has the right to choose his own religion according to his feelings or thoughts. As you get older, you start seeing life and also the religion in which you belong differently. That's the time when only *you* have the right to change your path. That's what I did too. I have chosen what I've considered to be best for my soul. I've chosen something I was truly connected with and the path I have needed the most.

Egotrism took birth out of many paths I've studied and some that I have followed. From studying, reading, experience, and maturity, to the people I have met and learned from, I took the best I got and put it all together. There were books, magazines, papers, and websites that I read with a clear mind. There were people that I have listened to with an open soul. But now I see experience and age were the most important. There were people who have helped me a lot along the way, starting from my character and attitude that they helped recover and correct, to even learning how to write grammatically correct, express myself, talk, think, and behave. A lot is still "under construction," evolution is ever changing and I am still young.

If your guess is that I have something to do with creepy stuff such as Satanism and Demons, you'd be right. These were part of my life for almost half of it, and still play an important role in it, just as Christianity and God were for the other half of my very young existence. How it all happened, I'll explain right now.

The "dark" faith (so to speak), embraced my soul 9 years ago. Since then I have been studying Satanism, with my soul and mind, with an appetite for knowledge, and a strong attraction, resulting from the spiritual connection I had with Satan since birth. Yes, I've always been spiritually connected to Satan, just as I was with Jehovah (God). Since I was a child I believed in God. We were very close and indeed He played a major role in my life. I have been a very devoted follower to both Gods, in separate times of my life. I always took religion and spirituality seriously for I knew and felt it's importance and impact in my life. I consider that religion has the role to help the individual to exceed any limit in his way, and to evolve both spiritually and intellectually. For that reason, I was determined to leave Christianity behind for the stupid thought that it wasn't giving me what I was needing at that time.

It is true, that while I was a Christian I was very anxious and frustrated. I felt spiritually empty and vulnerable, and compared to the period I have devoted myself to the Devil, I can say that the "dark" side helped me much more. What I failed to understand all this time, and luckily got it at last a few months ago, is that God was not responsible for the happenings in my life and that I was disappointed by myself and not by Him. I have expected from God what most people expect from an employee, or better yet, from a slave. It is true I haven't asked for money, a house, or a wife. However, like any man, I have asked for guidance and strength, and these two have been provided by Satan, psychologically explained through auto-suggestion, and spiritually explained through channeling.

I began to see Christianity, honestly enough, for what it really is. A religion that would keep me away from spiritual evolution. A weak religion, limited and without logic and spirituality. I've seen with my own eyes how religion can affect your way of life and thinking. I had been a Christian for about 10 years because I was forced to. My dad, who is especially a quite profound Christian, forced me to follow his religion, and that's what I did, but not with my soul. It was my soul that proved to me that this is a false, satiric, and revolting religion . I observed how Christianity can destroy your soul and mind. In my childhood, I went to churches and monasteries from time to time, and what I have seen there, simply shocked me. A bunch of people praying desperately to God, in vain, going to the altar and kissing a crucifix, which bears the image of a half-naked tortured man, and leaving their slobber on the cross until another one comes and puts his mouth on it. I was...totally disgusted. For 10 or 11 years I was constrained to swallow this religion.

Christianity, the religion of the people, is nothing more than a manipulating phenomenon for the weak. I've seen this and have given blame, unconsciously enough, to God, which I associated with this sickness represented by the Church and the Bible, forgetting my *personal* business with Him. There is a big difference between spirituality and religion, and the best example of this is the way God acts upon the adept, and the way Christianity does. I made the mistake to accuse them both.

In time, I've changed. Disgusted and anti-Christian to the bone, I've chosen the exact opposite. I chose Satanism, a religion that urges the adept to be confident, autodidact, intelligent; that urges the adept to be a fighter, not a slave.

Now, don't get me wrong.. I don't see Satanism as a refuge for those who are unsatisfied by God, or a revenge on the world and God, or like a plan B, and second choice. Hating God and being anti-Christian is, indeed, a satanic act, but for me that religion did not limit itself at this. It was far more than just inversed Christianity. It was far more than listening to black metal and screaming "Fuck God ! Hail Satan!" That is shit. You can look absolutely normal, you can act normal, you can listen to Shakira and still be a Satanist. What was most important, at least for me, was the relationship with Satan, which I had always wanted to get bigger and bigger. I wanted Him to be a part of my life, as God "didn't have the necessary disposition for that." I wanted to show the world that Satanists are far better than they think. I wanted to make Satanists proud when shouting "Hail Satan!" and knowing that others will not have anything to reproach them with or treat them as enemies, but as someone superior.

Indeed, anyone can be mad at God. Anyone can shout "Fuck God! Hail Satan!" Anyone can kneel and pray, do a ritual, etc. But *living* your life as a Satanist, dedicating every second of it to Satan and enjoying every second of it, trying to become better and better, showing the world that a Satanist is not a madman but a superior man, someone who can come in front of the world saying he is a Satanist without the risk of being mocked or attacked because he is too frustrated. All of this is what makes up the true Satanic follower. Compared to Christianity, I've seen this as the right path and followed it without objection.

This change did not happen only because I

loathe Christianity however. It was a reason, but not the only one. The main reason was that I was connected to Satan, just as I was with God. I knew who Satan was long before I ever heard of His name, long before anyone told me of such a figure. I always felt the presence of a higher entity besides God, but I never knew who it was until the age of 12, when I first discovered Satanism. I started to understand the whole picture, and the time had come when I decided to meet this entity personally and see what His plans might be for me. It was at the age of 13 when my life took a big turn 180 degrees and I began to call myself a Satanist.

When my father found out that I was a Satanist, he beat me…typical Christian. He couldn't accept it. But then, I didn't care, you see. There was no one that could change my path. I was fully dedicated to the god that I thought was always there for me; the only god that wouldn't keep me in chains, but would offer me liberty and knowledge, happiness and love. This was true to me for a long time until early this year, when I started having some experiences, and only by necessity, that I had to renounce the god that I have loved so much.

I was "godless" until my narcissism took over. I declared myself the Messiah of Myself, The Buddha of My Life. The Gods I've worshipped became now associates in spiritual work. Little by little, I've combined Them and Their religions, and put together what now I call Egotrism, the religion of the *self*, That which spurns any artificiality and scorns every part of weakness. A religion that truly urges the adept to be autodidact, confident, and *free;* To evolve spiritually, not weaken yourself, wasting your life, sad and "sinless".

That's what life is given for, to evolve and to enjoy all of its pleasures, whether it be mental, spiritual, material, or carnal. Why stay away from all of this, because it's a sin? Is it a sin to be free or to be happy? Is it a sin to enjoy all of the biological pleasures? Not for me. I do what I do. This path is not for everyone. It is only for those who really want it and think they can handle it. Don't like it? Don't buy it! Unlike other religions, you don't need to pray continuously and wait for an answer. This religion teaches you how to get things for yourself, be it physically, through magick, or any other method.

With the help of magick you can heal and destroy. Any man has the right to use it. With the help of magick and spiritual meditation, you open up a new world, a world in which you don't need to kneel in front of a false god to ask for food, or you have to fight to obtain what you desire. Through magick and meditation, you can find the power to advance, and to evolve from the rank of a worm on the scale of evolution to something grand. All of this and more, I was able to introduce and establish in Egotrism and give it birth.

If you ask me, I'd say that Egotrism is the religion of the 21st century. The only reason I invented this "religion" is because I needed it. It was because I had to form myself into a spiritual human being, and for that, I needed more than just words off of the internet, or from a book or a friend. I needed to get in touch with myself first to know the world around me.

It is a religion of the self and highly individual, in that it evolves at the same time with the adept as he starts to add things that come right with it. Egotrism is just that. It is a combination of many paths and systems, but all according to your OWN needs. It is a new religion, based a lot on the old ways, but does not limit itself to that.

I molded this religion after my own personality. While I am not much of a traditionalist, I do however respect tradition and use it when it is needed. However, I have often learned that the more "ingredients" you put into something, the better it will get. You just need to know the right stuff to put in and to know your tastes. The Egotrist does not follow any tradition, but rather creates his own tradition and belief. Unlike the orthodox Christian or the traditional Satanist, the Egotrist is a little more free to expand his practices and beliefs as he feels, and to borrow from more traditions and beliefs (i.e. Christianity, Satanism, Demonolatry, Chaos Magick, Sinister Path, Kabbalah, etc.) to create his own religion or type of Egotrism. It does not have strict beliefs to follow or a set of ideas necessarily. It's in a continuous evolution. It allows the practitioner to keep adding the necessary "ingredients" as he needs. You may say this is cheap stew, but for me it's favorite dish. It's healthy.

Unlike other religions or systems, Egotrism is very practical as it leaves you to deal a lot with life and puts YOU in the first place. No god, be it Satan,

Jehovah, Allah, etc. is more important than yourself. I have said that it's the religion of the 21st century and you'll understand why. Not only because it has the new beliefs, but because it relates to the problems that we deal with nowadays. Instead of blind faith it has proof, instead of mystical theories it has science, and instead of a dogma it has freedom.

In many cases it is different from most religions, including Christianity and Satanism. What it has in common with most religions though, is the presence of the Divine, which is not worshiped, but rather used as an ally in the works of magick. In Egotrism the Gods do not take first place in your life. Everything you do in life you do for yourself, not for Them. They may be your friends, spiritual guides, or whatever. You may want to thank them for their time, patience, and wisdom. But still, you are number one.

One who kneels in front of an altar asking for this and that is nothing but a beggar. An Egotrist does not beg. He acts, he does, he wins, in any way possible. We are the masters of our destinies, the Gods are our force!

All that we do, we do for ourselves and by our will alone. If you want to invoke Jehovah and feel the urge to do a Chaos Magick ritual in which you probably would have to invent another god, you do that. If you want to invoke Satan and want to communicate with the demonic spirits, you may very well dwell into Demonolatry. You are a Modern Magician, but that doesn't mean you can't do a 300 year old traditional ritual. There are differences but they all depend on *you*. I have my own EGOtrism. You can have one too, just be creative. There are no rules, only decisions that you make. There are only points you can follow and others that you avoid.

Some points I like to follow are the 21 Satanic Points. For those who aren't familiar with them, they are a set of ideas that can be found in the Black Book Of Satan by O.N.A. (Order of the Nine Angles). These are ideas for those who follow that which the O.N.A. calls "The Sinister Path", a quite different style of Traditional Satanism that has gained a lot of followers lately.

In my opinion these are ideas that every person who wants to be stronger and invulnerable should follow. Its what makes the life and mind of a true man. (Editor's Note: copyright laws prohibit us from re-printing those points here.)

Just like the 21 Satanic Points, one must create his own to build his life in a way that he can evolve. Either by using physical force, mind manipulation, or magick, he needs to destroy and create according to his needs for a better life.

Another important idea in Egotrism is balance. Not only in spirituality, but life in general. There's not much appreciation to the terms "good"' and "bad", only by the adept's perception of them and wish to take them in consideration. I've learned that being neutral is many times the best choice. There is never an "evil" without a "good". That's how nature is in fact.. balanced. And nature is a part of this religion. Such is the way of Egotrism.

UNDER THE SIGN OF SATAN
Alain Immortal Wolf

He dreamed about liberty and self-construction.
He lived in this world of slavery and mind obstruction.

He wanted independence and honor.
He was programmed for obedience and labor.

In this World of Xtian domination and blindness,
In this World of culpability and pain

Swear of allegiance, swear of revenge
Swear of loyalty , swear of liberty

Reject the abomination, the liar
Spit on the cross and the book of lies

The false teachings and the teachers
Reject the grave of life

Thou our Dark Lord he shows
Raise his fists, shout his swear

Thou Satan proud he stay
The Perfect warrior, The perfect Hero.

VISITATION
Alain Immortal Wolf

A night like any other
Dark and rainy

A boy was in his room to rest
His eyes where closed

Suddenly it smells like crap
Knocking and talking

You are mine...
Fear in the boys heart

So ice cold the room
Windows close

Wind inside
He appears - you are mine

Disappear like it comes
The boy knows his destiny

Never forgot this evening

Præy by Ovezt

Stasia O.

Age 40
Boston, MA
Actress

Like many, I was raised a Catholic. When I went to college, I began to notice conflicts in what I had been taught as a child and the reality of what was actually being done within the church. The forgiveness I was taught was not there and it became obvious that Jesus did NOT, in fact, love everyone. Later in my adulthood, I began to realize that I did not share the beliefs of the organized religions and there was no way I could practice any of them. I refused to believe something simply because a religion says it is what I should believe.

There was a point however, at which I briefly reconsidered the faith I had been brought up in. While going through an extremely difficult time that led into a clinical depression, I started going into a church several times a week (outside of Mass) to pray for help. I also had a list of prayers I would recite every single night before bed. My prayers were never answered – not one.

I had been intrigued by the occult and the darker path for years after seeing a talk show about spell casting. I began researching it a lot online and in books. I studied Wicca, Paganism, and other occult paths and even dabbled a bit here & there in different forms of Magick but I never had any success. I joined several occult message boards in search of answers and assistance. I was desperate for relief from my depression. I cast spell after spell after spell. Chaos Magick, Candle Burning Magick, Image Magick, Voodoo, Hoodoo. I know now that the reason nothing worked is because I never really committed to any one thing, and because none of those were right for me.

Then I began researching and studying Satanism. I think what attracted me the most (at first) was that the focus was ME and not some non-present God that was never ever really there. My beliefs, my truths, the way I live my life, Satanism just fit. I had long since given up on my Christian upbringing. It didn't take me long to decide that I wanted to dedicate and so I did. The moment I finished my dedication ritual, a warmth came over me and I became giddy with joy – I don't know how else to explain it – I actually had an uncontrollable outburst of laughter. I had never felt anything like it before.

The next day, I woke up with an overwhelming feeling that life was good and everything was going to better from now on...I just felt GOOD *and* HAPPY....for the first time in a very long time. I knew immediately I had done the right thing and I have never, ever doubted it or looked back.

My life has turned around completely over the past 5 years and for the better. Ever since I became a Satanist, my depression has been cured; my fears, worries, anxieties, insecurities, etc. have all but disappeared. I no longer feel alone, lost, or without purpose. My prayers are now answered, my rituals successful. I have a good life now, a better life. I achieve goals and have made many of my dreams come true. I am a better me. I believe that it is because I have finally found my true path in life and have stayed on it.

Brad Morlan

Age 38
Greater Toronto Area
Computer Hardware Technician

Growing up in a home where Santa Claus, the Easter bunny and the tooth fairy did not exist was not that unusual for me, until I started to realize other children in school didn't have the same practices and beliefs I did. I come from a small family. I am the youngest of 3 children and the only practitioner left of my family beliefs.

When other kids were celebrating Christmas or Hanukah with their families, we were celebrating the Winter Solstice, making holiday decorations to put on the Yule Log, saying special prayers for the coming year, and making plans for the coming Spring. I did not understand why other kids got school breaks for their holidays and we didn't for ours until I was a bit older and started to realize that our beliefs were not what people would call normal.

These beliefs and practices stem from my

mother's side of my family. My grandfather's family traditions are demon worshipers, Generational Demonolators. My grandmother's family are practitioners of Traditional Witchcraft. So this makes my mother's generation and mine a very unique blend of spiritual practice, however, the two work very well together.

I started my path at the tender age of 6, with my first initiation under the direction of Hecate, our family Matron. My sisters did not want to be initiated at all, they had no interest in our family traditions even then, but with a few divinations that my mother and grandfather had done, it was decided that I would be started down a path of priesthood to carry on the family rituals and traditions. I can remember being infused with the love of all things occult even then, and showed some signs of psychic ability, namely psychometry and clairaudience. So, I began a very structured learning process of magick and ritual usage from that age. It was a regimen of learning the elements and getting "in tune" with them, casting circles versus not casting them, and of course beginning to learn the use of magick appropriately.

At the age of 8, I was initiated as an Adept. I must explain what this means. In our traditions, attaining the level of Adept is a rite of passage that shows a certain magical proficiency that is demonstrated, and a certain amount of spiritual growth is attained. Also, this is a requirement to move forward into the priesthood, and allows one to preside over smaller workings.

This initiation was hard for my mother. She didn't want to see her baby growing up too fast, and also because she had fear that I had a big mouth! Which at that age, I pretty much did. I made the mistake one year of explaining to some kids in school that there is no such thing as the Easter bunny, that their belief in it was stupid because Easter was a made up and stolen tradition and I could prove it! Well, I recounted a story that my grandfather told me that my grandmother used to tell her children It was about the inquisition and burning times, and of people who were not so different than us. They were persecuted and forced to believe what the Christians believed or they would be killed, their rituals and practices were taken away from them, and perverted into what we now have today as Easter, Christmas, and such.

Needless to say, that did not go over well in the public school system. My parents were called, and I had to explain what exactly I said, and why. To keep silent at that age, was not my strong suit. I was subsequently evaluated by the school psychologist, and had to attend weekly meetings to make sure there was no ritual abuse in the home. Of course, they found no evidence of such, and we were let off the hook so to speak, however child protective services came in and threatened to take all three of us away from my mother. That didn't happen thankfully! From then on, I had to learn quickly why it is important to keep silent.

From age 8 to age 12, I learned more advanced forms of magick, and took my 3rd initiation, sort of a pre-ordination assisting priest. Now, I still had a whole lot to learn, but my grandfather was getting older, and didn't have the patience and drive anymore to keep up for much longer, especially since I wanted to know everything, and I wanted to know everything RIGHT NOW! Of course, it didn't happen like that, but I started my know it all phase a bit early. We went through a lot of material in those 4 years, from learning more energy work, ritual preparation, advanced meditation, more in-depth study into the elements, and wort-cunning.

I have always had an affinity for plants, especially in magick. My mother and grandfather taught me the way they were taught, which was to find the plants in the area where we lived, take samples, thanking the plant for the sample and knowledge it will bring by giving a drop of blood to the plant. The next phase of the process was to press the plant, but before doing so, connecting with the plants essence so I could learn more about the plant and it's uses not only magically, but medicinally as well. Then it went into a herbal of my own making, with the information I received from the plant and my mother and grandfather.

My 12th Birthday was the big day, the 3rd initiation. It was a joyous day, and a very difficult one. A task that I will never forget was doing a complete circle casting, and opening an elemental portal, in Hebrew. That was a challenge, and I studied for months on the language. One of my best friends was Jewish, so he helped me a lot.

31

After my initiation into pre-priesthood, things slowed down. My grandfather was almost 80, and his memory wasn't as good as it used to be, and that led to my own search for more advanced magick and learning. I came across "Ceremonial Magick," "The Goetia," "The Key of Solomon," and other grimoires that I devoured and poured over for more knowledge; modifying some of it (of course), and the parts that I could not figure out, I just left alone. My mother was a huge help, and supported me in my endeavors, giving me more bits of family information and lessons as I went.

My grandfather shared more knowledge as he could remember it, a lot of our traditions are oral. When I turned 21, my grandfather was 85. I was finally ordained, and admitted to High Priesthood. I learned more things that I had never known, because it was only for our priesthood to know. I also became owner of whatever family documents we have, and I have done my best over the years since, to add to it so that one day, I may find a suitable person to pass this down to.

My grandfather was a well-respected pillar of the community. He was a farmer and truck driver. Not the most glamorous of careers, but he provided well for his family for many, many years and my grandmother was a homemaker who raised 4 children, my mother being the youngest of them.

I never knew my grandmother in the flesh, she passed away when my mother was 15, 10 years before I was born. However, from a young age, I can remember her coming to me, and talking with me about anything from how much I hated the fact that I didn't have any brothers to, "Can I put a spell on my step-dad because he's mean!" and just about anything else in-between. My mother thought I had an imaginary playmate, even though I would call her grandma. We never discussed this until I was about 16, when she finally understood that it was her mother I had been seeing and interacting with all those years.

After high school, I went to college and got a degree in Computer Science, and have led a pretty "normal" life. I have had successful relationships with people of all religious faiths, teaching people along the way who want to know more of my beliefs, I am pretty open about them (without giving out too much information) and people seem to appreciate that. I am still a working magician to this day, and I still lead a pretty normal life. I have friends from all walks of life, and I am thankful every day for the life that I was given, and what I've made of it, even the hard parts.

Every day is a learning experience that I look forward to every single day. I am an amateur artist, I like to draw and paint, and have won several awards for my artwork. I am also a musician as well as computer tech. My family is very musically inclined. My grandfather played the trumpet and violin, my mother the piano and clarinet, and my sisters also played instruments. I learned to play the viola, violin, cello, bass, a little piano, the baritone, the flute, and the piccolo. But, my love is the stringed instruments.

People are always a bit shocked to find out

about my beliefs, because I don't look the part. Oh, I did when I was a teenager. I wore black clothes, had a mohawk, had several different colors of hair, had piercings, etc. but we are all just normal people with normal lives. As I get older, I look back at that time in my life and laugh. It was a lot of fun! People do guess correctly that I love horror movies, hard rock, gothic music, and "satanic" music. However, they also don't know that I love comedies, "chick flicks," Disney movies, and I love all types of music.

I am the last member of my family to practice our beliefs, however that has not made me lose sight of the bigger picture. While I don't understand fully why my immediate family abandoned our ways, it may be for the best, especially the ones who showed no interest at all. I still love them and we still have a pretty happy and stable family despite our new-found religious differences. We still fight like normal, and have disagreements, but, that's what people do. One thing my mother and grandfather always taught us, was that we had the right to choose. I don't regret the decision to stick with my family ways, and I hope that my other family members don't regret their decisions they have made about their new practices either.

Currently, I am living happily in Toronto Canada with my husband Cliff and continuing to write and enjoy living a wonderful life, getting inspiration from my beliefs, my surroundings and my spouse.

Balam **by B. Morlan**

(Reverend)Arturo Royal

Age: 39.
California, U.S.A.
Occupation: artist, writer, poet, musician, minister of
The First Eregnostic Church Of The Deep Light.
http://www.facebook.com/pages/Eregnosis/19248
3240840529?sk=info

I've always been of the Devil. Heretical ideas
are my life's blood. I never cease to ask questions,
even ones that most ignore. Simply thinking in such
a manner can be detrimental to health among the
beasts, but this is important to me. Most
importantly, I want to become more — physically,
spiritually, ontologically. I want to be truly
meaningful and significant to myself and others, but
mostly to myself. These are several reasons why
some come to the one who takes us not in but on,
really, not out of "paternal concern," but out of our
shared joy and lust for life, mirth, laughter, and a
good time, the one who's myth tells the story of
gaining the ultimate prize (that which is anathema to

any dictator: one's absolute freedom and true empowerment of our isolate self), Satan. This is my story....

Yours truly was born somewhere in Mexico, very south, and by an ocean. I was born in the seventies. Economic times got tough, so my family moved north. Although we were still living in Mexico, on the border town of Tijuana, it was then that I truly discovered the American culture via its favorite propaganda media machine – the television. The economy was shit there too, so we headed even further north: to America....

There I became more entrenched in the American culture. My favorite things about it were breakfast cereal, Saturday morning cartoons, and Star Trek. The cereal taught me how to get fat, how to merchandise, how to lie to get money, how to make garbage look pretty, even edible, and then sell it. The cartoons taught me that everything in life was insane yet hysterical, even death, and that I wanted to be a superhuman with super powers. Star Trek taught me...well, everything else I needed to live in America, including how to be Mr. Spock. Let me explain that last bit; to this day I give credit to the pointy eared one, for the way I got rid of my Mexican accent was by ceaselessly imitating Mr. Spock's flat patterned, American vernacular...take that as ye will.

Now living in the States, I noticed that all the Mexicans around me wanted to be rich. Being rich was the American dream. But after encountering the rich, the rich seemed as miserable as the poor, just richer. When I was six, I had what Buddhists call the vision of Dukka, which some translate as "sorrow" but a better translation would be "imperfection." I realized that following the pattern of going to college, marrying, having kids, a career, and then finally dying, that the American Dream, in short, was a total nightmare to me; a recipe for disaster to any true potential of creatures that hold all the secrets of the universe, literally, within our very quantum selves. This strange pattern meant that when the achiever of this "dream" finally dies, there won't be much left to bury, a waste. All the "stuff" that people wanted was not enough. Material wealth and a family were fine, but that wasn't all there was to it, at least not for me. So I decided that instead I was going to be an artist; to express ideas, beliefs, concepts, emotions, and to also capture that elusive dragon called life and "record" it via music, writing, images, and whatever I could get my little paws on. Not the answer to the conundrum of life, but it was a fine start. But first I had to become educated. I regarded artists as high class people, if a little mad, and high class people are educated people.

Education means lots of money and lots of books. Money would have to come later, but books I could obtain. My mother by then had left her ancestral faith of Catholicism, becoming a hardcore protestant, and forbade any literature other than the Bible. So of course I immediately disobeyed and began secretly reading Science Fiction books. (Shakespeare, and his ilk, always bored me. And after becoming much more literate, Shakespeare STILL bores me, but that's ok, because Stephen King and Carl Sagan bore me too.)

Finally hitting 18, I flatly denied Christianity and its ilk, telling my family so; and then stopped going to church and began reading everything I could. Interestingly enough, my mother seemed to understand my position the most. Although she, of course vehemently disagreed, she left me to my own devices.

The first victim was Raymond Buckland's Complete Book of Witchcraft, which was interesting for a while. I never thought of witches as nice folks. I plowed through. After vampirizing and saturating myself with what was Wicca in the 90's, I went for Crowley, of course. I got and read everything possible by him. The grimoires followed very quickly: "Grimorium Verum," "The Lesser and Greater Keys of Solomon," "The Black Pullet," etc. Then somehow I encountered Robert Anton Wilson and all the folks at Falcon Publications and went off into mind altering tangents galore. The Church Of The Subgenius followed to my shocked but tickled cynicism. Chaos Magick, Discordianism, Buddhism, Daoism, Existentialism, Gnosticism, Quantum Physics, Nietzsche, William Burroughs, Ciroan, Charles Baudelaire, Celine, world poetry(and I mean poetry from all over the world including the ancient world), postmodern philosophy, Marcel Duchamp, Surrealism, Da Da, comic books, Charles Bukowski, Camus, Clive Barker, Anton Chekov, Guy de Maupassant, etc., etc., ad infinitum. I read and learned so much I forgot who I was, what anything was, but I was as happy as a vampire in an all-girl Catholic high school with all its girls menstruating at the same time.

I performed rituals and weird things happened. I sat in meditation and experienced calm and focus. I threw curses to destroy enemies, explored the aether and gained money, sex, and some existential fun. Most of the (book) information I was getting, with the exception of Nietzsche, Foucault, and a couple of others, was very tainted with notions of becoming "one with the universe," of "losing the ego," and "selflessness." I didn't mind these at some level except that these doctrines were so overt it seemed like a con; an ensnaring if not an enslaving one; a con job that had gone unnoticed by the best thinkers, magicians, and sorcerers out there. Even the "darkest" Chaos Magick was plagued with these teachings. Everything seemed geared toward the "destruction of the ego," not really of becoming more but of becoming less. Intuitively I recoiled from all this. I dreaded the scenario, it made me nauseous. This filled me with guilt, as these doctrines say that if one doesn't destroy the ego, one cannot be an "adept," which is the goal of magick in most circles (no pun intended). What made it worse for me was that these teachings state that this "dread" is simply the "ego recoiling from the abyss" (whatever that means), so destroy my ego I must, because they said so.

But my ego was exactly WHY I came to alternative beliefs, philosophy, magick, etc. My ego was (actually, is) exactly what finally gave meaning to my life and my existence. Christianity the way I knew it, was a horrific way to perceive life, self, and others, with all its hate, bigotry, servility, fear, death, guilt... in short, the enslavement and the perversion of the ego. These other guys wanted to actually destroy it! But I wanted my ego to be appreciated, nursed, strengthened, cared for, as the fantastic, beautiful, meaningful piece of artwork that it is, as everyone else's ego is too if they take the time to make it so.

Ego simply means "self" after all, it doesn't mean hubris. My ego had taken years to build and make usable as part of my body/mind complex. The ego, to me, means the best and only tool to experience life with because it isn't "limited." It is most flexible, expansive, and multidimensional, a multiplicity as much as it is a unit. Sure, we use the body to experience life too, but without an ego, a "self", the body lives in a state of limbo, neither here nor there, without the ego (self), the body is insane or animal at best. Why would I want to destroy such a creature? I was shocked and in the end disgusted. So I decided to do what any regular old joe like myself would have done. I told that doctrine to go eat dog titty and I chose to be for the ego, to be an egoist as well as an artist.

To this day, it is my firm belief that these teachings about the destruction of the ego have grossly mistaken their semantics. In other words, they were dead wrong. I think that by "destruction of the ego" they actually mean the "crap" of the ego we don't need anymore, things like conformity and much of what were indoctrinated with, but not the ego (the self) itself. Among the many teachings of this ego killing doctrine, some meditation practices claim to aim at "obliterating the ego." Well, if one's aware of the said "ego obliteration," the "ego" is still THERE to observe it, for nothing else observes.

Those who have claimed to have accomplished such a task and have thusly become "adepts," and for all their proclamations, they divulge all too human shortcomings, and in most cases this more than anything. I'm all too human myself, but the key here is to try to be better and not make unrealistic claims. As a perfect example, Aleister Crowley, that "high magus" of the ages, was a heroin addict, somewhat of a con artist and a bit of an asshole. He may have been a very intelligent, talented, prolific, innovative, creative person and a great sorcerer, but not the paragon of an "ipssissimus". These might seem like simplistic conclusions, but this is only in the interest of brevity. Make an objective research on the matter for yourself and see what you come up with.

Inside me somewhere there existed the postulation that somebody had gone terribly wrong with their semantics. Someone somewhere, sometime, had severely fucked up. Possibly in tangent with that, some opportunists may have used this ego killing canon to manipulate disciples, thus perpetuating the confusion. The first part of my ego emancipation came from my own observation and intuition, the second part came when I discovered Satanism.

Unfortunately in its early years, around the time of my discovery, much of the modern Satanic literature was full of petty anger, hatred, conveniently "edited" Nietzschean concepts, and lame elitism–in some instances it still is. Many of their groups are riddled with cults of personality, and in some instances, it still is. The overt materialism and simpleton philosophy began to quickly get on my nerves. The Satanism of that time had for its basic philosophy an ironic version of Marxist realist-materialism with little patience for magick and mysteries. My mind, especially the artist aspect, loves metaphysical and ontological complexities, mysteries and symbols, "old dusty books" full of magical seals and recipes, as well as anything "space-age," Sci-Fi, "materialistic," and hardcore scientific, thus forcing me to clash with most of the overtly bland Satanic philosophy and outlook of those years.

Additionally, the concepts "weak" and "strong" – notions that riddle too many Satanic treatises to this day – are, like "good" and "evil," extremely arbitrary (don't believe me? Again, research for yourself, I'd like for people to think more so than to agree). The constant invocation of these two dichotomies, in the aforementioned Satanic works, seemed more a weird juvenile desperation on the part of these authors than anything very useful as a philosophy for living among others. Though I must say that their embracing of "Satan" – the ultimate heretic and individual, the very model for "evil" according to oppressive individuals and dogmas – and their placement of the ego above all else, was a great inspiration and a new shift for the better in my path.

Others understood that the "destruction of the ego" was utter bullshit, and this helped propel me even more into my path of "selfullness" (a neologism I coined to use instead of the heavily loaded term, if you'll pardon the redundancy, "selfishness").

In the end I came to realize that all I had to do was pick and choose what I liked and discard what I didn't like, and, as Tubal Cain did, forge my own Satanic path, and make Satan my own.

Much time passed before I fully owned Satan, the adversary, and Lucifer, the light bearer, the ultimate individualists…challenging, prosperous, driven, generous, and wise. I wanted to embrace a spiritual path, a way of living and perceiving; a religion, if you will, that incorporated a philosophy in which the person, the individual, the self, the EGO, is the last and only true arbiter of its own destiny, its own way. Not only that, but this ego could be molded, stretched, expanded, exaggerated, shrunk, loved, educated, multiplied, etc, in any way to become more than what it was from the "perceived" so-called beginning. I wanted this, I CHOSE this. And this religion wasn't about exclusion of others based on any ridiculous elitist notions. It was about embracing myself in all my complexity and totality, truly and unabashedly, without shame or guilt, and becoming more with it all. That is power. But this isn't about puerile hubris at all. We all possess and are possessed by that awesome and beautiful raw material: the ego, which is the self. This "religion", this way, I call Satanism. There's more to you, go now and make it!

Faceless by Lex

Joshua Brunson

Age 16
Parker, Colorado
Student

Religion has been something of an enigma for me, a complex problem I have yearned to solve for quite a few years now. It took many a transition, many a day of learning and comprehending, but I think I may have finally come to a close on my personal religious affiliation, and oddly enough, it turned out to be what many would refer to as "Satanism."

When I was younger, I think beginning of birth to roughly my eighth or ninth year of age, my family was whole and we were Catholics. I wouldn't say we were strict, but it was prominent in daily life. It was prominent (and still is) with relatives and we actively participated in the local Roman Catholic Church. As a young child, I also attended Sunday school which led up to my first communion and my first confirmation. Aside from going to church and Sunday school, I also attended a private Catholic School (two, in two different states) from kindergarten to first grade. My experiences with Christianity were largely negative. I didn't feel as if I could inquire about things that baffled me. I didn't feel as if the answers I received were substantial, and I just felt largely odd practicing that religion. I felt like I didn't belong with the religion, like I just thought differently from others, but it was what my parents practiced, it was what everyone I knew followed and said was "right," and so I did as they told me to do.

After my eighth or ninth birthday (I can't recall which year specifically), my parents got a divorce and I ended up living with my mother and sister. My father moved to Arkansas and my mother to Houston, Texas. While transitioning to Houston, my mother wanted to become an Orthodox Jew. Personally speaking, I felt nothing much with Christianity, and the change didn't make me feel odd or unhappy. So we did, and now we were Orthodox Jews living in a Jewish community for a good three or four years. While in this community, I became a student at Robert M. Beren Academy, a Jewish private school that went from pre-k all the way up to 12th grade. I attended this school from 5th to 7th grade, along with attending a Hebrew School on Sundays, where I learned some of the Hebrew language (my knowledge of which is incredibly rusty, as is my French). I met and befriended a few close individuals, but yet again, I didn't feel anything with

Judaism. I also disliked some of the community for my own reasons, and some of the homophobia that existed in the community that I simply couldn't understand. I was an Orthodox Jew until 13, after my Bar Mitzvah, and then my family moved to Parker, Colorado.

I stayed with the Jewish religion until I turned 14. That was when I began to drift away from all things Jewish. I understood the religion, including some tales of demons and some myths and legends involving some of the demons. I understood the Halacha fairly well, and I had attended hour-long study sessions with one of the community's Rabbis on Saturdays. I also attended Yeshiva Hakayitz in Chicago, Illinois for a summer. In the end, it just didn't fit me like how Christianity didn't fit me – it simply felt odd to me, it felt unnatural and forced. I held fear of the god, not reverence, not respect. I felt that fear was present too prominently; I felt that such fear fueled the discrimination present in the religions and so, I decided to do away with religion and become an atheist.

Atheism didn't treat me well either. In fact I was more of an agnostic than an atheist. However, as an atheist, I still looked into other religions (Islam, Buddhism, LaVey Satanism, and Wicca) and none of those religions felt right. LaVeyan Satanism was what actually drew me, partially, to learning about theistic Satanism. The History Channel also helped with this curiosity, as did the movie "The Rite" (oddly enough) and so, I explored theistic Satanism. When I read the articles I found online by one Diane

Vera, I felt more comfortable than when I read articles done by Christians with a Christian view, or Jews with a Jewish view. I felt that I had found a religion that wouldn't be discriminate towards me based on my sexual orientation (gay), and a religion that seemed to attract a good number of levelheaded people who, at the very least, had common sense for once. Through Diane Vera's website, she recommended reading The Complete Book of Demonolatry by S. Connolly, and so I did.

Demonolatry is a religion that has most definitely piqued my interest. The book S. Connolly wrote feels like it's written by someone who is respectful of differing beliefs, someone who holds respect in a high regard. I also took note that the religion itself seemed to be heavy on respect, and it doesn't see the world in absolute (good/evil). That's what primarily drew me to Demonolatry, the mentality of the religion and the writings I have been able to read by those who are Demonolators. At my time of writing this, I'm no initiate (or, pre-initiate), and I'm definitely not the most well-versed in the religion, but I see it definitely as something worth looking into more. The religion makes sense to me. It makes sense because the followers aren't being held by the shackles of fear and guilt, they aren't being discriminated, nor are they actively discriminating against others. It just makes sense to me that respect should be shown to any entity that holds a mentor or teacher relationship with an individual. It's a religion that, from what I have read and have processed, promotes critical thinking and promotes science, while other religions (like Christianity) go on to refute science (I've seen Christians do this, look at the old Flat-Earth Society, or the explanations many Creationists hold to refute evolution with).

Satan and the plethora of other daemons just make more sense to me; it's hard to articulate in words as it's sort of a feeling, like a "click" in the brain, if that makes any sense whatsoever. The only thing I find a downside to Demonolatry is how hard it is to find like-minded individuals to ask questions, to get clarifications from, and to observe and learn from. However, perhaps my luck will change with this endeavor and I'll be able to perhaps talk to a current Demonolater and get a better understanding of what's involved with the religion.

From my experiences in many different religions (Christianity, Judaism, a brief stint with Buddhism, research into Islam, LaVeyan Satanism, and looking into Wicca) I haven't found any such religion outside of the "Satanism" umbrella where the majority of members I do see, and the books of which I do read, contain not only knowledge, but the proper common sense to convey and put that knowledge into practice. Plus, the not-so-judgmental feel I get from the writings of a number of Satanists, Demonolaters, and Setians is yet another reason why I feel particularly drawn to this branch of religion.

Again, I am currently more interested in Demonolatry than I am in the Temple of Set, or other groups, largely because of what I've read and come to understand from what I have read. It's more to do with a "this feels like it would fit me pretty well," than anything else.

However, I'm just as normal as any other person, except that I don't speak of my current religious affiliation, for I know that people will make a big deal out of it. I don't tell even those closest to me, as I do know that they will not understand and likely will not strive to understand. When it comes to applications for jobs, applications for schools, and for some programs, I don't state my religious affiliation – I just label myself as atheist. It's a pain and a drain to go through every day, essentially lying to others about what I believe in fear of being barred from opportunities, and even in fear of being barred from participating in some weekend games. Or possibly barred from participation in a volunteer Search and Rescue/leadership training program due to the local squadron being hosted in a church, and I'm sure if my religious affiliations popped up, I'd be removed. People in my life, and possibly in the lives of many others, don't strive to learn what a burden it can be to simply not be of the norm in some cases – especially when falling into a misunderstood, misrepresented affiliation.

I get fairly good grades, I've received awards for my work, I get above average marks on tests such as the PSAT and the practice ACT. I have aspirations to go into the service, and to possibly become an author in the future. I'm not planning global domination/annihilation from the comfort of my couch.

I'm not some rebellious teen, what do I have

to rebel from? I am given quite an extraordinary amount of freedom and I understand why I have this freedom. I definitely don't do things to intentionally piss off the person who has given me such freedom. Some would say I am just in a "rebellious" phase. I have been told that in the past. If I was in such a state I would be broadcasting it to my family, not hiding it, not studying it, and not thinking about it, or writing notes in relation to it, or writing my own understanding of things down on paper. I wouldn't have taken the time to write this; I wouldn't have had nearly as much to say. I most definitely would not have looked towards other groups under the Satanic umbrella, nor would I have delved much into anything.

In the end, I'm just your average ordinary, un-extraordinary gay American teen.

Ellen

Age 20
Tucson, Arizona
Full Time Student

My family is pretty normal. I was blessed to have both my parents in my life, happily married, but there were occasional hardships like anyone else. I grew up in a Christian household and I even went to Catholic Church a few times, but for the most part my parents couldn't decide on raising my brother and I as Catholic (my mother's side) or Pentecostal (my father's side), so we never really learned much about Christianity at all. I've now learned that my parents weren't married in a Catholic church and took my brother and I into consideration, since having their marriage validated by my mother's church would have meant my brother and I would have to go through all the bells and whistles that come with Catholicism.

Early on I had a wild imagination. Twice, when I was eight, I had some interesting incidents occur involving the weather. I wished for snow and it snowed in April. That never happens in Arizona. Another time when it was raining I told my father and brother "it'd be cool if it started hailing right about now!" and seconds later, flecks of white ice began hitting the car. I didn't ever try again, nor am I suitable for meteorological studies, but along with thinking I saw a ghost in my room (I'm now pretty sure it was a dream) it was my first exposure to the things I couldn't explain.

Around the age of twelve I found a book about various witches and magicians (I now know that book was a work of fiction), as well as a book about herbal remedies on the living room shelf and I took them and looked at them. I was mystified. I then explored Wicca, but I didn't find what I was looking for. When my parents found out, they told me it was "evil" and handed me the Bible and told me to read it.

They fed me horror stories about how some of my father's friends tried to evoke a Demon and all ended up dying. They warned me it was a portal better left unopened. They blamed one of my father's co-workers for letting me speak to her daughter, who was a few years older than me. I felt like these were all excuses, but this was the first time they showed any discomfort about a topic. They knew I was bi-curious (and accept me as bisexual now) and have otherwise supported me in my choices.

The one thing that stuck out about that "talk" we had was something my mom said. My ancestors were Mayan on my mother's side of the family, so she wasn't surprised at my interest in magic or nature.

Christianity just wasn't for me. I couldn't understand it or accept it. I read about Shinto (to no avail) in the hopes that maybe there still was a religion out there for me, but it didn't feel like the right fit either. I had no goals in life, didn't expect myself to make it to college at all. I was at a loss for words and becoming bitter about religion in general until I discovered Demonolatry right before I turned fifteen years old.

One day I had the urge to type in "Satanism" into Google. It led me to the OFS website somehow, and I read about Demonolatry. It was like a switch turned on in my head. I tried to join the OFS forum and was re-directed to the now-defunct teen OFS forum. What I could find and read about the topic made me feel happier, more outgoing, and I noticed a dramatic reverse in how my life was going.

I overcame social phobia for the most part, made a ton of new friends, and suddenly went from a non-existent GPA with the possibility of repeating a grade to applying myself academically and graduating on time with a 3.2GPA. I'm not making an outrageous claim that Demonolatry made me smart, or convinced my teachers to make my grades better, for those doubting this feat. Demonolatry and Satanism gave me a new found optimism, and working with Demons gave me that extra little push to apply myself more often.

The teen forum closed down shortly after I found it. I continued to study Satanism with the help of one of its more active members, James, and we keep in contact to this day for the most part. He has taught me a lot, and helped me to realize that Satanism and Demonolatry weren't a teenage "fad" for me. He suggested amazing books to me that have furthered my studies dramatically and kept me from becoming a Church-defiling delinquent. I owe a lot to him for being an extremely huge mentor along my path. He's now let me "fly freely" at this point, but still gives me a stern word or two if I make a mistake, or words of praise if I do something that surprises him.

All in all it wasn't as much trying to "rebel" against my parents as much as trying to find something that was missing. I never really dated a lot until college, so loneliness might have been part of it, but I just couldn't accept Jesus as my lord and savior. Plus, there was no way I could rebel against my ultra-accepting parents who didn't send me away to "pray away the gay" when a friend told them I was interested in both men and women. My loving parents let me dye my hair pink, get a ton of piercings, and signed for a tattoo when I was seventeen (which has the sigil of Lucifer hidden in the design. He's the first Demon I worked with). They constantly tell me how proud they are of me, even when I showed up with a second tattoo on my wrist a couple months ago.

All of these things were allowed because I was a pretty well behaved child and didn't do anything without thinking things through. I never partied and I only tried weed once and told them about it. I dressed modestly of my own accord; I've only ever heard "you will not leave the house dressed like that" once, in kindergarten, when I tried to wear a short skirt over a pair of pants because it was cold and I wanted to wear a skirt. That's why I'm not quite sure why religion is such a touchy subject.

It was only after I turned eighteen that I started veering away from calling myself a Satanist. The connotation of that word is very negative. I sometimes feel like James is a little miffed about it, but labels mean nothing as long as your heart is in the right place. Satan is still part of my pantheon, as well as Demons from the Dukanté and Goetic hierarchies.

If asked my religion, I'd also like a chance to describe it briefly so people can get a better understanding rather than saying "So you like upside down crosses and black metal?" "You're going to Hell you poor child!" or "I never would have guessed from the way you're dressed." I did go through a black wearing phase in late middle school through early high school, but I think it's safe to say every teenager goes through some kind of phase during that time.

If you saw me on the street now I'd be just another face you're soon to forget. I have about eight ear piercings I don't normally wear jewelry in, and I'd rather dye my hair natural colors these days. I mind my vocabulary in public, try not to be disrespectful, and keep to myself unless spoken to.

I've had a couple of elderly women talk to me on the bus and say it was nice that I was a "good Christian girl" because many people in my age group are petty, impertinent, or downright rude. If only they knew, huh?

I can often be seen on the bus with a heavy pink backpack I've used since my senior year of high school containing sketchbooks, books about Russian and/or books about Spanish. Or you'll see me online playing video games with friends, offering my artwork for commissions or posting pictures on my Facebook that aren't distasteful or drunken party scenes. I post on the OFS Forum, now called the GenDem Forum, as "Laith".

I'm not mysterious or particularly exciting in the least, I'm just living out my life peacefully, as I hope others do the same. Oh, I might also be covered in cat fur from time to time. I love animals, too. They're not my familiars or any kind of sacrifice subjects (I would never think of hurting an animal!); my cats are some of my fondest friends. In fact, one's sprawled out across my bed right now.

I would like to think I am very successful; not in terms of money or fame (which honestly neither of which mean a lot to me), but Demonolatry has helped me find the diligence to pursue my talents. I received a student of the month award in high school as well as the "most improved" in my beginning choir. I auditioned into the women's ensemble (I'm still surprised I made the cut) and competed around the state.

More recently I'm about to start my third year of

college. I am a member of Phi Theta Kappa honor society, I have a 3.8 GPA , putting me in the top 10% of my class, and I am studying hard to become a translator. I have exceeded my own expectations in terms of drawing (a passion I've had since I was three), and even got commissioned by PGA Golfer Marc Leishman's fiancée for a wedding portrait.

I'm ready to take on the world since my story has yet to completely unfold. I haven't told my parents about Demonolatry, but as I said before, I typically think things through, often for years, and it'll take a quite a few more years before I'm ready.

Dexter by Ellen "Laith"

Cassaundra (Cassy) Donovan

Age 29
Harrington, DE
Retail sales/student

Even at birth I was a passionate fighter (though it would be much later in life when I would understand why and who was behind it) coming out of my mother's womb at a mere 1 lb. 12 oz; I also came out of her an incredible 3 months early. Obviously, I had a hell of a lot of problems because of the fact that I wasn't fully developed. My medical issues were so severe that doctors predicted that I either would not make it or if by a slim chance that I did, I would never be able to walk or talk. Some of my numerous complications included water on the brain and a collapsed right lung. I also suffered from jaundice, and my stomach was so underdeveloped that doctors had to insert a feeding tube that went around my brain and traveled from there down to my stomach. If blood needed to be taken it was done from my ankles because my veins kept collapsing. An incubator was my home, unless of course I was undergoing one of my many surgeries.

On a number of occasions I had actually died on that operating table due to complications though I was always brought back. Many of the doctors began referring to me as a miracle baby. Upon arriving home, my mother would dress me in doll's clothes because nothing else would fit my tiny frame. All in all, I came out of that traumatic experience unscathed, save for medical scars and cerebral palsy due to the lack of oxygen that my brain received. Even this form of the condition is very slight and the only outward sign is that I walk with a limp, other than that I am quite a happy and healthy individual.

Since around the age of 13 I had always felt a dark and welcoming presence around me. This presence began to manifest itself in the dark arts and the occult. Thus, I began my search for what this presence exactly was. In my later years, my mother would mention to me that this was around the same time that she felt (and still does to this day) that I was demon possessed. My search began in the usual manner, when I began delving into LeVayan Satanism. This was the only book available in the mass market that was easily attainable. Upon reading the text, I was left with the feeling of "that's it." This was clearly not the tome that I was expecting and my intellectual nature was left yearning for more. From there I delved into dark witchcraft and again was left unsatisfied, for even though it held a darker tinge of gothic, it still held all the usual trappings of fluffy bunny Wicca. Various authors and tomes followed, from Michael W. Ford and Luciferian Witchcraft, to Don Webb and the Temple of Set. I finally found my niche and came home in 2009 when I delved head first into Demonolatry.

It was there that I could finally put a name to the fiery, intense, and passionate presence that had been surrounding me since very early on in my life. It was my Flereous, and from then on our relationship would only continue to grow and flourish. The love that I had for him would only deepen with time. I do not run a coven/sect and prefer instead to have Flereous be my teacher/guide and work alone with him. My unending devotion and praise of him comes in the form of a daily ritual, prayers to him during the morning and evening hours, nightly meditation to spend time in his presence, and of course the annual rite to Flereous. On the night of the Summer Solstice in 2009, I officially dedicated both myself and my life to my Flereous. I have his sigil tattooed on my flesh and shall forever wear his seal on my left hand as symbols of my undying devotion and love to him.

It is quite apparent, based on my studies in the occult, that I have always been on a quest for knowledge and that I am very much like a sponge. This particular aspect of myself branches out into my everyday life, as well as with my college endeavors. Ever since I was a child I had always wanted to become a psychologist. I have always held a strong fascination with the brain and mental disorders, and at this early age I planned to make these dreams a reality. What can I say? I'm a lass with some very serious goals and ambitions.

After completing high school in 2000 I enrolled in Delaware Technical and Community College and by 2005, I had received an Associate's Degree in Human Services. I had also graduated with honors in the Phi Theta Kappa National Honor Society (yes I am a nerd). By that Fall I had enrolled in Delaware State University in the Social Work Program, and in 2007 I had successfully completed and earned a Bachelor's Degree in that field.

Currently I am taking a break from college and working at Wal-mart in the apparel section in order to raise enough money so that I may go back to school and attain a Master's Degree in Community Counseling at Wilmington University. I also have a long term goal of a PhD in Psychology. I plan on using my degree to offer individual counseling to others in need.

...from beneath Flereous' blackened wings,
Cassaundra L. Donovan

Martin McGreggor

Age 26
St. Louis, Missouri
Entrepreneur and Small Business Owner

Eighteen years old, knelt before a shin-height makeshift altar. Nothing before me looked particularly expensive or impressive. That wasn't supposed to be the point though. Everything had been chosen for functionality, for purpose. John traded a sideways glance with me as we lit our candles. It had been a long road for us, and I don't think either of us expected our feet to carry us there. It truly is perilous business, stepping outside your door.

I was born into a Baptist family, and for years, even after I had recognized the church for what it truly was, I felt a strong impulse to be a man of God. To be a good person, and seek forgiveness for the things I had and would, do.

Forgiveness and belonging comes easy in Christianity. All one must do is - nothing. Don't be human, don't be strong, and above all, don't be inquisitive. (Unless it's Inquisition time, that is!) That is a matter for another story, however.

To return to the matter at hand, John had also come from a similar Christian background. Brought together by shared life experiences, home lives, and very similar principles, we had been friends for a few years, and were now roommates. Looking back now, years later, at the deluge of coincidences and bizarre occurrences in both of our histories that lead to our eventual friendship, there is little doubt that Satan's hand was at work, for I do not believe either one of us would have found Satan, if it were not for the other. When we did discover Him, it was completely by chance on our part, and neither of us had really given any thought to Satanism. If anything, the contrary would have been closer to the truth, with both of us abandoning the Judeo-Christian dogma and belief systems long before. But we both succeeded in following a simple direction we were given when we began our research: "Before reading anything else, truly attempt to forget everything you have been told about Satan. Forget all the assumptions and preconceptions you have, and enter the subject with an open mind." And after doing so, we began to read…for months.

As I have already stated, John and I had been friends for a few years prior to the night in question. Many nights before it we spent in independent study, both of us researching our own areas of interest, and bringing particular things of interest to the other's notice. We immersed ourselves in the subject matter…the creation of man; the religions of the ancient pre-Christian civilizations; meditation and magic; Demons, rituals, and rites. And as we studied, it soon became apparent that these were not the evil, corrupting, abhorrent beliefs that we were led to believe in during our Christian indoctrination.

Instead, we were reading about self-empowerment and improvement, strength of will and mental discipline, dedication and loyalty. A Human belief system that didn't make it a sin to be human. Something that put emphasis on the mental, spiritual, and emotional health of the follower, instead of the fanatical adherence to an unhealthy code of conduct in order to gain entry into some kind of mystical "No Girls Allowed" tree house in the sky after death. Satanism replaced abstinence and blind faith with personal responsibility and accountability. We had both found our new home.

And so the time had come. We began the ritual and when the time came, took turns reciting our prayers. We had very little money, so the tools at our disposal were limited to what we could find in the house. I started, standing before this altar of pieced together miscellany, and a sole black pillar candle, brand new, which constituted what little money I did have. I renounced the Christian God and I spoke of dedication, loyalty, and service to Satan. John arose in front of a candle of his own. He spoke of strength, self-empowerment, and service to Satan. If I'm not mistaken, afterward, we both liked the other's dedication more. After we spoke it came time to sign our name on the dotted line so to speak, both in ink, and in blood. What should have been the simple end to the ritual, turned into a personal test of my resolve, which I will never forget. For Satan is a tester, without a doubt. John was able to cut his finger quite easily, dripping a bit of blood onto his paper. I however for some reason, could not get the knife to cut my finger. Try as I might, the knife just would not penetrate the skin. Fearing that I may have slipped into a state of sub-conscious "pansy," I handed John the knife, who proceeded to push the knife down on my finger extremely hard. Hard enough for my entire finger to turn white from the pressure. Still, nothing. After a few tense moments, he looked at me and said, "I don't know, man. I'm not sure you are meant to do this..." and with a resounding "Fuck that!" I took up the knife again and restarted my work. Able to open a small cut in the skin of my index finger, which still wouldn't bleed, I proceeded to put the blade of the knife inside the cut and wiggled it back and forth with a little "sawing" motion. This finally gave me a resounding sting and blood welled up onto my finger. Placing a few drops on my paper, I smeared it into a signature line (stupidly, with the same finger I had just cut, which re-acquainted me with that same stinging sensation) and signed my name in ink directly on the line I had made. We burned our dedications, and sat at peace for some time.

The years following our dedication rite have been full of even more tests from Satan. We've had good years and bad, seen good times and sad ones. We've known the struggle and challenge of daily self-empowerment and what it means to actively work to better oneself. We've had our dire moments and times of personal struggle, when all we wanted was to go back to when things were simpler and easier; when nothing more was required of us than doing what we were told and not asking questions. But as Thomas Paine once said, "A mind once enlightened cannot again become dark." As Lucifer the Light Bearer, the Morning Star, illuminates our path – never again can we fall into the darkness that is ignorance, blind faith, and unwavering thoughtlessness. Faith is meant to have belief in something despite a lack of evidence, not belief in something despite overwhelming evidence to the contrary. Satan expects more of us, and so should you.

Martin McGreggor
Ut Servo Diabolus!

Sentinel

Age 45
Maesteg, Wales, United Kingdom
Mathematician with interests in Paleoclimatology
(Ice Ages, why they happen, and when is the next
one?) and Martial Artist.

It's been a strange road for me into
Demonolatry. I first became interested in the occult
at the age of 15 when I tried a Ouija Board. It
worked very well, but I think I was pestered by
something afterwards, and have never done anything
with a Ouija board since then. Things lapsed then
until I was about 22 when I discovered Prediction
Magazine here in the UK. I was very much into
Wicca and white magic (now very fluffy bunny).
During that time I was very keen to find a copy of
"The Exorcist" on VHS in the UK (it was banned
then). I read in a horror magazine that it was Pazuzu
who possessed Regan. At that time, I came across
"The Necronomicon" (Simon), and discovered
Pazuzu in there along with a sigil. It chilled me to the
bone. Then I got a copy of "The Exorcist." For

some reason I felt that Pazuzu had been unfairly "picked on." Something didn't weigh correctly in my head.

Jump forward now to around 1997. I see a television program on "The Satanic Bible." I order a copy - it made so much sense to me. My mother introduces me to a used book seller in our local market. He had a copy of Fred Gettings "Dictionary of Demons." About 1999, I came across Tezrian's Vault and book called "Modern Demonolatry" by S. Connolly. I order myself a copy from the UK. I was sold. Everything made so much sense. I read it and read it.

June 2001 - Open Heart surgery, a scary time. Not much chance of a chaplain in the hospital talking to me about the demons (in a good way anyway). July to September was spent recovering from surgery.

October 2001 met my soon(ish) to be missus. She took me to Malaysia (she is Malaysian) in 2002. Went to a Ganesh temple. Not one to poo-poo others religions, I tagged along and was invited to join in (strange sense of power in that place). Anyway, married July 2002 and got dragged off to church for midnight mass Christmas 2002. My wife was quite fond of Catholicism (as well as Hinduism). I had (shamefully) forgotten about the demons at that time, and even started accompanying Bina to church more often.

2005 – My wife was diagnosed with cancer. I felt lost. Went to church on her behalf more and more often.

Then a turning point came. I had thought of converting to Catholicism, even going to some meetings. I talked to some people. A voice asked me "What are you doing?" and essentially I got the feeling "What about us? Have you forgotten?"
My feelings for converting to Catholicism went quickly - very quickly. I felt as if I had been "saved."

I still balance Ganesh and the Demons. I continually read S. Connolly's "Complete Guide to Demonolatry." I ALWAYS discover something new, either about myself or Demonolatry. I spend many hours philosophically contemplating issues raised by reading the book. I feel quite "safe" for want of a better word. I still do not have a matron or patron, but I do have my favorites, Pazuzu being one of them.

My wife and I have an acceptance of each other's religions. Her altar is down stairs, with some Catholic stuff and some Ganesh stuff on it. I will light an incense stick for Ganesh sometimes. My altar is upstairs. It has various statuettes (Pazuzu, Bast, Baphomet, inverted pentagrams, etc.), a scrying mirror, offering tray, etc. and my wife respects it totally, even asking questions sometimes.

Demonolatry has brought a sense of completeness to me.

~Sentinel, October 2012

Tenebrae Accedit

Age 44
Adirondack Mountains, New York State
Traditional Witch

Hmm… where to start.

When one is asked to write something such as this, it is tough to try to decide which experiences will be shared with the reader, and which will be left out. Sometimes a lot of small experiences lead up to larger ones, etc. I will try to do my best to not leave any stone unturned, or to leave you with questions in your mind, nor do I want to bore you. So that being said, let me begin my tale of my journey onto my spiritual path.

I was born in 1967 in a small town in Northeastern N.Y. to Native American parents, and naturally, I grew up learning about nature; plants, trees, animals, etc. I was always taught to pay attention to everything around me, no matter how insignificant it may seem. I was told "The Great Spirit speaks to us in many ways, every day, we just need to pay attention."

Throughout my years of growing up, I always did just that. Paid attention. Little was I to know that all I paid attention to and learned would be one of the best things I ever did in my life.

Many nights I listened to my father and mother talk about "up home." This was the reservation they grew up on in Northeastern Canada. They told me stories of their upbringing, how our people lived, etc. This helped to spark my interest in other cultures and how their people had many similarities to my people. Social Studies fascinated me at a very young age. Ancient Egypt, Sumeria...The Norse, Germanic, Norwegian, and Celtic tribes, and even other Native American tribes...the list goes on. Where am I going with this? You will soon find out...

I had also heard stories of religion, spirituality, rituals, and magic; how all things have a spirit, etc. This fascinated me also. Did all these other cultures believe in the same types of things? I set my mind to find out. We lived across the street from a church, which I attended, but my parents did not (Yes later). I wanted to know, so I asked the pastor. I was told no, it is against the will of God, and evil. I asked my Social Studies teacher. I was told yes. I was confused. I promised myself that one day, I would know the answers to these questions.

In the midst of all this, I watched T.V. programs that mostly dealt with the same topics. I also watched programs/movies with witches, sorcerers, etc. Prominent ones I can remember were

"Winsome Witch," "Bed knobs And Broomsticks," "Bell, Book, And Candle"...the list goes on and on. One day, after dinner, we watched a program (I forget the name) in where the people of a small town had gypsies come into town. The townspeople treated them badly. The town had been having a drought, and tensions were high. The gypsy leader told the people that his mother could help. She would "pray" for rain. He went back to their camp, and told her. She walked out of her Vardo, went to a tree, cut off a branch, then cut some of her hair as an offering on the ground at its base, drew a circle with the branch, waved the stick in the air at the four directions, reciting some words at each one, then to the middle, and did the same, which took a little longer than the rest. She retraced the circle the opposite way, then left the branch in the middle. Thunder, lightning - it started raining!!

I was awed. I immediately took my scissors, and went outside in our backyard. I copied what she did, as best I could. It was cloudy already, no lightning, no thunder, but it started raining as soon as I was done. I was in the rain, looking up and laughing, my mind reeling, thrilled with what I did and the result. My mother however, was not happy. She grabbed me, kneeled down, and said sternly "Don't you ever do that again!" Although I had gotten in trouble, I was smiling. Magic was real, and I knew it.

This is the first time I have shared that story with anyone other than a few of my students and my wife. My mother never told anyone of that day, including my father, who would have been extremely angry. He wanted nothing to do with any of that. The nuns and priests on "the rez" scarred (and scared) him badly. My mother owned a Ouija Board and a Kreskin's ESP Game, which never came out when dad was home. To this day I don't think he even knew she had it. If I asked, she would get them out to teach me about them, but when dad was on his way home they "disappeared." My older brother would come home, and would sit with us. I found out mom had taught him too. I also found out that he read Tarot. I wanted to learn this also, so he started teaching me. I was 12 at this point. My brother was a good enough teacher, that at 13, I was doing readings on my own.

At around the same age, I was introduced to Led Zeppelin and Black Sabbath, two of my brother's favorite bands. I saw magazine pictures of them, and looked at their album covers. Intrigued by what I saw, I asked my brother about the symbols and artwork. He told me they were into the occult. He explained to me what it was and I was blown away! Now everything had a label, so to speak. This was the spark I needed. I started getting books out of the village library about anything and everything to do with the occult. My main focus, and what fascinated me the most, were witches. The only books I could find on them were about devil worship, etc. I didn't care. The occult was evil. I didn't care. It was against what I had learned in church. I still didn't care. I kept reading.

There were no bookstores or internet here

when I was young, so I really had to dig to find anything. Whatever I found I wrote down in notebooks. As I got older, I found that four of my friends had the same interests, and they did the same thing. We started getting together and sharing notes. This was not an easy task when we entered high school, because the librarian monitored what we were doing while we were in the library. One day, while on an occult search, I decided to take a harder look through the reference section for the umpteenth time. I went to the back, and scanned the shelves. I saw something that caught my eye. My jaw dropped. A complete set of "Man, Myth, And Magic" encyclopedias! I started flipping through them, and couldn't believe my eyes.

When I told my friends, they reacted the same way. We then formulated a plan where one of us would join the AV (Audio Visual) Club. Then we would have access to a copy machine, and copies for free. We put our plan into action. It worked perfectly. We now had tons of info that we needed. We had already been using and practicing with all that we had found, but these books expanded our knowledge of the occult, mythology, magic, and how it was all tied together.

Soon after, I found out why the pastor had told me what he did. I found out it was because of Christianity that these things had been suppressed. People, and in some cases, whole cultures, their beliefs, and history were erased. When I talked to members of my family, I found out my people suffered also; they were told to convert to

Christianity, or God would punish them. Later, these same priests gave them "gifts" of blankets for the cold winter ahead. They were infested with smallpox. I was angry - very angry. I had been lied to. I made a promise to myself. I was never going to church again.

One of my friends had a cousin who lived in New York City, and he came up from time to time. He was 2 years older, and into the occult, but didn't know about us. We decided to call him, and tell him, in the hopes he could help in some way. The next time he came up with his parents on vacation, he would bring up some things for us to see. When he finally did come up, he brought some books: "The Book Of The Law", "The Satanic Bible," "The Lesser and Greater Keys Of Solomon," etc. These books, among a few others, were the first actual occult books I had ever seen. I was 15 then. We had already decided to work together at this point, and had already bonded ourselves together magically. We pooled our money, bought these books from him, and went from there. This was how we acquired our books from then on. We used these books until a couple years after graduation, when life took four of us in different directions, and one to an early grave in an alcohol related crash.

I was alone now, but lived on my own with my girlfriend. I still practiced, but she didn't know. I had a car, and was able to find books and info easier. Still no internet or bookstores, but I was still searching. I had been playing guitar since I was 13, and through the years, met a lot of local kids my age that played. A lot of us kept playing and kept in touch after we finished school. One day after jamming with some friends, we went to the drummer's house to have a few beers and hang out. While I was there, I noticed some watercolors he did of some Tarot cards. When everyone else had left, I stayed and talked to him about them. We were the same age, and started at the same age! We talked about the occult long into the night, shared stories, and he showed me his books. Among them were "The Satanic Bible," and books on Druidism, and Stonehenge. He and I had done the same things... the searches, the notebooks, etc.

We decided to begin studying together, and started looking for bookstores. We found one 12 miles from where we lived. It had an occult section, but they called it "New Age." We looked, and found books on Witchcraft (Wicca). We flipped through the books. Hmmm. It was a legal religion. We bought the book "Wiccacraft" by Gerina Dunwich, and dug right in. We bought the book in May 1993 and initiated on Summer Solstice the same year. The only problem we had with Wicca, was all the stories we had read about witches doing black magic. We felt there had to be an explanation. So, a new search started, which covered some 16+ years. I started actually searching for Traditional Witchcraft 4 years ago (this being Oct. 31, 2011 as I type - what a great time to share this story, right?) on the internet, and found a lot of info online, as well as ordering books on the subject.

That search started my path onto Traditional

Witchcraft, which I practice now. I had a hard time believing that witches were all good, no bad. I was right. In Traditional Witchcraft, you do what needs to be done to get the job done. There is no 3 fold law, or a Rede. Curses and bindings, when justified, are used, and there is a dark side. I like to say that *"Traditional witches go where angels fear to tread."*

I have studied many different occult subjects through the years, and still do. Voodoo, Hoodoo, Pow wow, Ceremonial Magick…the list goes on forever. I have practiced some, and like to have a working knowledge or at least an good understanding of how the others work. I like to call them "magical systems."

My current study is Demonolatry. I have always been fascinated by Demons (thanks to the Goetia), and found info on it accidentally when looking on different occult websites. My current project at this time is writing my own Traditional Witchcraft Tradition, which will include Demonolatry.

All these years, my path has kept me very busy. I have been running a coven since 1993; teaching classes on assorted occult subjects since 1994; my girlfriend was initiated into Wicca in 1994; We were legally hand fasted in New York State in 1998 (we have been together since 1985, and are still together), and we were ordained as ministers by the Universal Life Church in 1999; and we do readings, spell work, teach, give advice, and do counseling on a daily and weekly basis. That list goes on and on also.

Through all of this, and a lot more trials and tribulations not spoken of here, I have trodden the path of the occult. I have always had a soft spot for the darker things in life. If you feel the need to do the same, by all means do it, but study first. Learn. Search. Practice. It is not something to be entered into half-heartedly, and for those of you who fear the dark, I leave you with this, my favorite quote:

"It is better to light a candle, than to curse the darkness."

But now I must go. I have a holiday to celebrate!

Happy Hallow's Eve.
Tenebrae Accedit (Darkness Approaches)

Laura Naysmith

Age 35
Glasgow, Scotland
Student

The purpose of this book is to show people that Satanists and Demonolaters are just regular people. So who am I? Well I'm a just your average Scottish, vegan, gay, dyslexic student of Theology and Religious Studies who happens to have a sideline in Satanic Clergy work. I'm not scary at all, honest. This is my story.

I have been a Theistic Satanist for going on six years or so. The one person who is mostly responsible for this is Anton Lavey (and Satan obviously). This of course is not unheard of within occult circles. Say what you like about Lavey, and I've said plenty about that man, he was someone that opened many people's eyes to a thought process that changed people. I first discovered him when I was a teenager and read an article in a magazine about the

Church of Satan, an organization that for me, was hugely fascinating, and still to this day continues to fascinate but for different reasons. Most of my teen years were spent not really knowing much of anything regarding Satanism, but really wanting to for an unknown reason. I was a regular attendee at church. Our church was the Church of Scotland, which is protestant and does not have a huge rhetoric regarding Satan, Demons or Hell. It's there but we don't really talk about it. Regardless of rhetoric, I still had the belief that Satan was evil and was to be feared, but this didn't seem to sit right with me for some reason, because I was starting to feel more drawn to him and really wanted to find out the truth, or at least the truth for me. I couldn't figure out why I was attracted to this "evil" deity when I wasn't an evil person myself. In truth, I would rather do you a good turn than a bad one, and as we all know, people that follow Satan are nasty, child killing, animal sacrificing nuts, right? So I decide to face my fear.

I decide the best thing I could do was pray. I thought "what have I got to lose?" so I prayed to Satan for the first time. Thinking if he really does exist then he will answer me, if he doesn't, oh well. He did answer me, not in a big booming voice saying "LAURA, I DO EXIST" but more in a suddenly knowing what to do, like an intuition kind of way. I had asked for guidance in learning more about him and other believers. I was guided to the internet, where I put in the longest search question ever, as I never had the right words to make it shorter. So I put something like "people who believe in the real Satan and who worship him." Now thinking back, that was daft but it did the job. I found the website The Joy of Satan, which was full of very interesting articles about Spiritual Satanism. I didn't agree with a lot of what was written (and that was way before I found out about the Nazi stuff), but it gave me more information to make further searches easier and shorter. Sure, Satan could have given me the info I wanted, but he likes us to have a go at it ourselves first, he just gave me a wee push in the right direction.

Finally, I found a site that reflected my views (what they were at that time) only they explained them in a more intelligent and eloquent manner. That was the Church of Azazel site run by Diane Vera. Through that site I came across her own web pages and yahoo sites. As my own self questioning continued, I realized that this was not the theology for me. Trying to find a theology and taking it for my own continued for a long time and it began to irritate me because I felt like I couldn't make up my mind.

Now looking back, and having FINALLY settled on a theology I'm comfortable with, I see a reason for this. If I had found my theology right away I would never have looked into others and I would have had a very narrow view of Theistic Satanism. So the journey (as irritating as it was at time) that I had gone on was necessary. I do believe that Satanism can be just as susceptible to schism as other religions, and it is only by understanding other's beliefs that we can avoid this, or at least not make it such an issue.

Okay, so by now I had explored the Joy of Satan and The Church of Azazel, tried on their beliefs for size, and found that they really didn't fit, so I was really back to square one (well sort of). After all, I now know that it is possible to have a theistic belief in Satan and that I wasn't the only one, but where do I go from here? Well it's obvious; Wicca is the way to go. Really? Why didn't I think of that before? After all it's a nature based religion, they strive to make the world a bit of better place and they have a representation of one of their Gods that sort of looks like Satan is supposed to look. Perfect.

So I became a student of Wicca. In fact as my studies progressed I called myself a Wiccan Satanist because I loved the practice of the rituals, the celebration of the holidays, and I love the god lore, but if I'm being perfectly honest I never really like the whole 3 fold law. I had Satan as my God figure and for me it made sense, but it was still a little bit unfulfilling. And of course there was the whole "not really fitting in anywhere" because Wiccans may be Pagan and are not supposed to have Christian beliefs (well apart from the Christian Wiccans), but they still seem to have the belief that Satan is evil. It was frustrating. But at least now I knew what I was looking for worship wise, so after a time my status as a Wiccan Satanist was diminishing and that was fine, because clearly I didn't need that part of my life anymore. I believed then and still believe now that things come into your life when you need them and they leave when you don't. I began to plod on just myself and letting my intuition and Satan be my guide.

One day I was surfing the net and came across a site all about Demonolatry. Suddenly it was like someone switched on the light in a previously pitch black room. A nature based religion that had ritual and special holidays and no 3 fold law. I loved that it didn't set itself up as a religion. That was all good, because that is such a high pedestal to fall from, and we have seen the problems the "good" religions have caused, and it certainly wasn't all bad either. It was neutral and allowed its adherents to take an action that they thought was justified, regardless of whether it would seem the "right" action in the eyes of someone else. Get angry if you need to, do good if you want to, but make sure either is justified. I ordered the "The Complete Book Of Demonolatry" and have read it from cover to cover several times since. Now I can honestly say that Demonolatry is the foundation of my own personal religious practice. But I am more comfortable talking from a Theistic Satanist perspective as I don't feel qualified to do justice to Demonolatry in that way.

Of course just because I now have a religious belief that can be put into words does not mean that I had all the answers, and sometimes I still found that I went back and forth on certain subjects, such as who Satan actually is. Is he a monotheistic god and there are no others? Is he one of many? Is he a fallen angel who rebelled against the Christian God? I also found that I relied a little too much on other's opinions in helping me to form my own. I kept needing reassurance and would double check with people I respected, to see if their experience was similar to mine, and if it wasn't, I would think my experience wasn't a true one. Thankfully, I no longer do this. I don't regret I ever did it, as everything is a learning process, and that process has been instrumental in shaping who I am as a theistic Satanist and has helped me with my vocation.

In 2006 I became ordained in the Universal Life Church after having realized that Satan has called me to become one of his clergy, which does sound totally "out-there" and possibly a little deluded. Since the ordination I have been involved in outreach work, which involves answering people's emails regarding Satan and their relationship with him. I've found that my own struggles and questions have helped me to help others who are going through the same thing. People sometimes just like to know that they are not alone.

I have a website and a YouTube channel both of which get steady traffic and interesting comments. I sincerely believe that Satan chooses his own; this is not a unique thought in Theistic Satanism but a popular one. He reaches out to his kin in many different ways, and with the arrival of the internet, people are finding other ways to discover their true self. As clergy, I can help to make the transition a little easier - hopefully. One thing the internet has done for Satanists is bring us together, and for people meet others who are like them. Many people are lucky enough to meet off-line as well as on, but even an online community is incredibly important and can be a life line.

There is very much a live and let live attitude to gender and sexuality within the satanic scene. I have talked to many transgender people who have found a peace within the satanic scene, and there are many openly gay men and women, myself being one. I have not been subject to any homophobic taunts, etc. from any Satanist. That's not to say that there aren't any homophobic Satanists of course. But it makes a nice change to be among religious people who you know will not judge you because of your sexuality, whereas in my day-to-day life, I am surrounded by Christians (I'm studying Theology and Religious Studies) and the potential is always there for one of them to react unkindly to my sexuality. The first year of my university course, I was condemned to hell a few times, and lost count of the amount of times I or gay people in general were called abominations. Satanism does not do this and it's a breath of fresh air. Satan has helped me to overcome the internal homophobia I felt about myself, and has shown me that who I am is who I was meant to be. I love the fact that he has shown the same thing to others too.

When it comes to actually telling people about my religious beliefs, you could say I am in a glass closet about them. The information is there if you look. A quick Google search will tell you what you want to know, although it may be a bit outdated. I very rarely make a special effort to tell people, but if they ask, I will just say Pagan. If they inquire further I will tell them. I do use my real name on anything that I write because I want to show that we do exist, and that the things you know or think you know might not be actually true. I'd be the most rubbish Satan worshipper in the world, if it was mandatory that you had to kill animals, hate all other religions, blaspheme against the Christian God all the time, etc. In truth, I couldn't give a bugger about what religion you are, if you have any at all. I judge a person on their own actions and words, not of those who happen to share a religious belief. Why do I want to waste my time bad mouthing Jesus and the Abrahamic God when I could be putting that time to better use by praising and worshipping my own Deities?

For my university work I have been very lucky to have been able to put my own interest in Satan to good use, and have done a couple of essays and a class talk on Satan. Granted, they were from the Muslim perspective of him, but I find that endlessly fascinating anyway. My dissertation topic is based on the role that Demonology has played in the growth of the Abrahamic faiths. It will be a negative portrayal of Satan and the Demons because it will be coming from the perspective of the religions that do hold him and the Demons in contempt, but without him and them where would they be? My own personal beliefs about Satan and the Demons does not stem from my previous Christian background. Sure, it started that way, but as I grew in my beliefs, I began to see that (for me at least) they are older than any of the Abrahamic religions and have been used as a pawn in their own game. So the dissertation should be interesting.

So that's my story; the story of a Satanist from Scotland, who, like most people with a religious belief, is just trying to muddle along as best she can.

Marie RavenSoul

Age 40
Toronto, Canada
Writer

It was not so much that I chose Satan… but that Satan chose me.

For as long as I can remember, I have felt a presence with me - an essence suffused with strength, darkness, and wisdom. As a child it was somewhat intimidating but also comforting at the same time. Satan was guiding me on a path that would lead to the ultimate decision that I would make in the summer of 1985- to follow him with my entire heart and soul.

Very early in my life I became curious about things of an occult nature. I would look through books at my school library that had to do with ghosts, witches, and extrasensory perception. I made my own Zener cards to practice my psychic abilities, and even though I wasn't proficient with them, I had a pretty good ratio of correct answers versus incorrect ones. In time I began to feel drawn to the darker aspects of things - horror books, death, dark artwork. At nine years old, I started to write my first 'novel's' main character - a vampire. Until this time I had no religious upbringing, but then was introduced to Catholicism through a family member, yet that didn't stop the progression into darkness that had been set for me. The gates were opening little by little.

At eleven years of age, I had a powerful experience when on a school trip to a cemetery. My teacher thought the best way to teach his class art and some history was to take us to as many cemeteries across Toronto that he could. On one occasion, when entering the cemetery, we saw a gravestone with SATAN written across it with red spray paint. Everyone was scared but I was in awe. Something about it being there at that exact time resonated with me and I could not help but stare at it even after everyone else had moved on. It just so happened that my teacher took a picture of it, yet out of all the pictures that he took, it was the only one that never developed properly. A few years later, I had told my friend's psychic aunt about the experience and she got the strongest feeling that Satan used the gravestone to let me know that he was with me. There was no escaping his call.

As I entered into my teenage years, I became very drawn to Satanic symbols; whether it was a pentagram on an album cover or an inverted cross drawn on the side of a bridge, they stirred feelings in me that I could not explain. It was soon after that I began to write a novel about a Satanic coven. I had no idea about such things but I wrote from my heart and what I felt was right. Little did I know at the time, but Satan would lead me to a coven a couple of years later. One night I had a very powerful channeling experience where a Demonic entity spoke to someone through me. I can't say that I did not feel apprehension, as something like that had never happened to me before, but it confirmed that Satan was protecting me and teaching me things about his nature, as well as aspects of myself.

Satan had been looking out for me for a very long time and preparing me for what was to come. He waited for just the right time to reveal himself to me to an even greater degree. It was a gradual process. I didn't wake up one day and decide to become a Satanist, and I didn't listen to a song or read a book that made me think Satanism was the religion for me. The decision to become a Satanist came from my experiences and what I had learned about Satan all the years proceeding, and at fourteen years old I made the commitment to follow him. I knew that was where I belonged, and Satan gave me such a powerful desire to learn as much about him as possible, so I sought to learn more. The first books I read were "The Satanic Bible" and "The Satanic Rituals" by Anton LaVey, and they encouraged me to dig even deeper as well as practice my Satanism. I wanted to live what I believed, not just have ideas floating around in my head. I got into black metal music, which was a great inspiration to me and my spiritual path, yet I must stress that *it was not the music that got me into Satanism*, but the Satanism that got me into the music. Bands like Mercyful Fate, King Diamond, Bathory, and Venom sang lyrics that penetrated my soul to such a deep level, and Satan used this music to give me strength at times when I had very little.

Dreams have always been a means in which Satan has communicated with me. A few months after I became a Satanist, I had a dream that I believe was my initiation. It was so powerful and intense that I can still remember details of it to this day- an old cathedral, people in black robes, and being led to the front where I would be given the mark of Satan. Following this, Satan became everything to me…my greatest desires were to commune with him through prayer and deep contemplation. All I wanted was an altar and to surround myself with Satanic images and words, but living at home and only being fifteen, I was limited in what I could do. After it was realized how serious I was about my beliefs, and after I continued to explain the importance of actually being able to practice my religion, I was given permission to construct an altar. It was an outward affirmation of what was going on within, and what I needed was to perform rituals to Satan and become closer to him.

In the 1980's being a Satanist meant, for the most part, being alone. Unlike today, unless one knew people who were also Satanists from the same geographical location, one could not commune with people of like mind as we can do today with the internet. Places like Yahoo groups, chat rooms, and social networking sites did not exist so it was close to impossible to meet other Satanists, unless you just happened to bump into them somewhere. Resources on Satanism were also very limited. Books by actual Satanists were practically non-existent and I did not have the luxury to turn on a computer and learn from others. Yet it was a special time...one of solitude, where I was able to focus solely on Satan and listen to what he had to teach me without anyone or anything getting in the way. Satan used one specific text to speak to me in a very powerful way and that was the Al-Jilwah. Certain verses would stand out as if Satan were saying the words directly to me, and preparing me for what lay ahead. As I always say, Satan is the best teacher and I would not trade that time of my spiritual journey for anything.

Satanism became my life. I could not get enough of Satan or anything that had an association with him. It did not matter if what I watched, read, or listened to was favorable to him or not, all I wanted was to hear about him some way, somehow. It was a hunger that could not be satiated but became stronger each day, and I could not contain what I was becoming. No one could hold me back from expressing my devotion to Satan through how I dressed and the jewelry I wore, and despite the "Satanic Panic" that had the media alarming everyone of the so- called crimes being committed in the name of Satan, I refused to hide who and what I was. Even though people thought Satanists were baby and animal killers because of what they were being force fed by Christians and others, I walked with pride because I knew who Satan truly was and I knew who I was. I was fortunate to have teachers in high school that listened to my side of the story and were very accommodating when I would bring up my beliefs in class. Yes, I had some negative experiences with other students, but instead of letting them bring me down, my belief in Satan grew stronger and nothing really mattered but him.

Nothing can compare to Satan's magnificent presence, and while other people my age were hanging out at the mall, I was writing poems about Satan. Through them, I expressed my love, devotion, and desire to be with Him for all eternity. I realized that it was through writing that I could best serve Satan in this world, and I could feel in my inner being that it was what Satan wanted. I dedicated myself totally to Satan and renounced my previous religious affiliation. I drew an inverted cross with my blood at the bottom of the written promises I had made, and placed a pentagram ring on my wedding finger to show that Satan would always be most important in my life. I was home. Satan became my god, my teacher, my muse, and always…my Father.

As time went on, things started happening that I did not understand at first. People talk about spiritual battles and while many scoff at the idea, I know all too well that they occur. For quite a few years, the "god" of the Christianity I was brought into when I was much younger, finagled and used much manipulation to pull me away from Satan. Satan let me go, and perhaps even encouraged me, to enter the enemy's domain. This was so I could know the enemy and his followers better, and I would learn the things I would need later on in my life. Because of this, I know the bible quite well and can show Christians and others the true nature of their god, and I am able to help others going through the same struggles. The Christians I came to know during that time were always afraid of Satan, and deep down they knew I was his. Although it was not an easy time, it was a testimony of Satan's awesome power and love for his chosen.

I came away from the spiritual struggles a much stronger Satanist. I learned more about Satan's wisdom, his knowledge, and his power. He taught me to overcome fear, guilt, and weakness, and to embrace his dark essence fully. Through the hard times, he gave me the courage to go on and inspired me to be the best I could be. I began to develop connections to the Demons which expanded my knowledge and perceptions of things. I experienced the motherliness of Ashtoreth, the vengeance of Abaddon, the deep wisdom of Ronove, and the healing touch of Verrine. As an expression of my devotion and to honor the Demons, I have gotten tattoos of many of their sigils and constructed altars to many of them in my home. It is only one of the ways that I practice my Demon worship and communicate with them. I had another initiation that took place in a dream, much more powerful than the first. It led me deeper into darkness, and made my connection to Satan much more concrete and eternal than it ever had been before.

In 2003, I became involved in the online Satanic scene and got to know other Satanists from across the world. I learned that many of them had gone through very similar experiences as me - both good and bad. It was evidence of Satan's majesty and his desire to have a personal connection with each of his chosen, and that he rises above the Christian god in any battle. As a result of my struggles, I started a group on Yahoo called "Spiritual Conflicts" in 2005 as a means for Satanists and others of the left hand path to share and discuss the struggles they themselves were facing; and then in 2006 I formed the group called "Satanist Friends," also on Yahoo, so Satanists of all different traditions could dialogue with one another. To honor Satan I created the website "In Satan's Honour," on which I express my feelings towards Satan through prayers, psalms, and poems, and I have included articles and devotions I have written to inspire my fellow Satanists. I am also the publisher and primary writer of "The Serpent's Tongue" webzine which I founded in 2009. Its purpose is to celebrate all things that are Satanic and dark and to be a unique voice for Satanists to share their beliefs through many different means.

Just recently, I created the group "Toronto Satanists" as a way for Satanists who live in Toronto and the surrounding regions to be able to discuss our beliefs and other matters pertaining to Satanism. As a result of that, the Toronto Satanist Meet-up was formed by a member of the group which she hosts every month. It has been my growing desire to make a difference for Satanism and the people who revere and worship my dark lord.

In conclusion, although Satan had chosen me first and guided me along the path to where he would reveal himself to me, I in turn, would choose to follow this magnificent being. I admired what had been written about his strength… him standing with fierce desire to be everything he wanted to be, and having a pride in himself that everything in existence envied. Knowing that he would encourage me to emulate him made me admire him even more. Being able to have the freedom where I could express what was within me, and where I could strive to become more than I could ever imagine, all because of his gift of the knowledge of good and evil, was something I could never be grateful enough for. No longer would I have to deny my true will. I could be with Satan forever in this life and in the life to come.

♥

Reading List

Dear Reader, this is by no means a complete reading list. It is merely a compilation of some pithy beginner friendly books regarding the subject of darker minority religions and magickal practices. Use this list to explore your curiosity and see where it takes you. – The Editors

Daemonolatry:

The Complete Book of Demonolatry by S. Connolly (DB Publishing 2006)

Luciferianism:

Beginning Luciferian Magick – Michael Ford (Lulu 2008)

Atheistic Satanism:

The Satanic Bible by Anton Szandor LaVey (Avon 1976)

The Satanic Paradigm by Winter Laake (Lulu 2011)

Theistic Satanism:

After much discussion we could not come to any agreements on good beginner books regarding theistic Satanism just because while there are numerous books on the subject out there, we didn't think the available ones did the subject justice. There just isn't a well-written, concise, thorough book about the subject out there. So you're on your own here.

Traditional Witchcraft:

Call Of The Horned Piper by Nigel Aldcroft Jackson. (Capell Bann Pub, 2001)

Masks Of Misrule by Nigel Aldcroft Jackson (Capell Bann Pub, 1996)

Treading The Mill by Nigel G. Pearson (Capell Bann Pub, 2007)

Traditional Witchcraft: A Cornish Book Of Ways by Gemma Gary (Troy Books, 2009)

A Witch Alone by Marion Green (Thorsons, 2002)

CPSIA information can be obtained at www.ICGtesting.com
Printed in the USA
BVOW06s1809260616

453530BV00016B/125/P